Henry Thayer Drowne

Genealogy of the Family of Solomon Drowne, M.D. of Rhode Island

With notices of his ancestors, 1646-1879

Henry Thayer Drowne

Genealogy of the Family of Solomon Drowne, M.D. of Rhode Island
With notices of his ancestors, 1646-1879

ISBN/EAN: 9783337318451

Printed in Europe, USA, Canada, Australia, Japan

Cover: Foto ©Lupo / pixelio.de

More available books at **www.hansebooks.com**

GENEALOGY

OF

THE FAMILY

OF

SOLOMON DROWNE, M. D.

OF

RHODE ISLAND,

WITH

NOTICES OF HIS ANCESTORS,

1646 — 1879.

BY HENRY T. DROWNE.

————◆————

PROVIDENCE:
PROVIDENCE PRESS COMPANY, PRINTERS.
1879.

THE DROWNE BRANCH

OF THE

RUSSELL FAMILY.

———◆———

SOLOMON DROWNE, M. D., born in Providence, Rhode Island, March 11, 1753, married November 20, 1777, in Holliston, Mass., ELIZABETH RUSSELL,⁵ (daughter of Thomas Russell,⁴ and Honora [Onner] Loud, of Boston). She was born April 16, 1759. Both died at Mount Hygeia, in Foster, Rhode Island ; he, February 5, 1834, and she, May 15, 1844.

Their children were :

   i. SOPHIA DROWNE, born March 11, 1779 ; died in Providence, June 20, 1784.

   ii. ELIZA RUSSELL DROWNE, born December 31, 1781 ; died in Foster, April 30, 1865.

  iii. CORNELIA DROWNE, born September 30, 1783 ; died in Foster, January 26, 1847.

  iv. SOPHIA DROWNE, born June 6, 1786 ; died in Providence, October 29, 1786.

   v. SOPHIA DROWNE, born October 9, 1787 ; died in Foster, August 29, 1816.

  vi. SARAH DROWNE, born September 10, 1790.

 vii. WILLIAM DROWNE, born October 26, 1793 ; died in Foster, June 15, 1874.

viii.   SOLOMON HORACE DROWNE, born August 24, 1796 ; died
in Woodstock, Connecticut, July 14, 1848.

ix.   HENRY BERNARDIN DROWNE, born April 6, 1799 ; died
in Providence, February 7, 1873.

The daughters of Dr. Drowne were all born in
Providence.

Solomon Drowne, M. D., was a great grandson of
Leonard Drowne,* who came from the west of England
on the accession of Charles the Second, and whose grave
is in the old Copp's Hill Burying Ground, Boston,
Massachusetts.   His grandfather and father were also
named Solomon, and his mother, Mercy (Tillinghast)
Arnold, was a granddaughter of the Rev. Pardon
Tillinghast, of Providence, Rhode Island.   He graduated
at Rhode Island College, (now Brown University,) in
1773 ; studied medicine, and received medical degrees
from the University of Pennsylvania and from Dart-
mouth College, New Hampshire.   Dr. Drowne served
as surgeon for several years, (1776–1780,) during the
war of the Revolution, in various hospitals and regi-
ments, and was in Sullivan's Expedition upon Rhode
Island.   In the fall of 1780 he went on a cruise as
surgeon in the private sloop of war Hope, his journal
of which, with the genealogy of his family, has been
printed.   He won the regard of Lafayette, the Counts

---

*LEONARD DROWNE, the ancestor of the Drowne family, was born in 1646, and car-
ried on ship building at Kittery, Maine; but in consequence of the Indian wars removed
his family and business in 1692 to Boston, where he died October 31, 1729.   His oldest son
Solomon, born January 23, 1681, was a ship-builder at Bristol, R. I., where he died October
9, 1730.   The grandson, Solomon, born October 4, 1706, settled in Providence as a merchant
in 1730, and for half a century bore a prominent part in the affairs of the town, which he
represented in the General Assembly.   Dr. Manning, of Brown University, writes that he
" found him one of the pillars of the church on his coming to Providence."   He died June
25, 1780, and was much respected for his strict probity, his sound judgment, and other
sterling traits of character.

de Rochambeau and d'Estaing, as well as of other
French officers, to such a degree, by his medical
ability and skill as a surgeon, that the chief of the
medical staff entrusted their invalid soldiers to his care
when they left for home.

In 1783 he was elected to the Board of Fellows in
Brown University. A year later he went to London,
and spent several months in travelling over England,
and in visiting the hospitals and medical schools. In
May, 1785, he visited Holland and Belgium for similar
purposes, and then went to Paris. While in France, he
was often a guest of Dr. Franklin, at Passy, in whose
society he met Mr. Jefferson, and other distinguished
men. On his return to Providence, he resumed the
practice of medicine ; but, in 1788, journeyed to Ohio,
and resided for nearly a year at Marietta. While there
he delivered a funeral eulogy on Gen. James M. Var-
num, (whom he had attended in his last sickness,) and
also the first anniversary oration on the settlement of
Marietta, April 7, 1789. He was also present, partici-
pating with Gen. St. Clair and others, in the Treaties
at Fort Harmar, in 1788-9, with Corn Planter and other
Indian chiefs. Returning to his native town he continued his practice until 1792, when, in consequence of
impaired health, he removed with his family to Morgantown, West Virginia, stopping en route to see Gen.
Washington, at Mt. Vernon ; and, in 1794, the danger
from border incursions of Indians being over, he went
to Union, Fayette county, Pennsylvania, where he lived
seven years. In 1801, he retraced his steps to Rhode
Island, and a little later settled in Foster. He called
his place Mt. Hygeia, and here he resided the remainder

of his days, devoting himself to professional duties, to his botanical garden, and to his scientific, classical and literary studies.

Dr. Drowne filled several public offices. He was in 1811, appointed Professor of Materia Medica and Botany, in Brown University ; and in 1819 was elected a delegate to the convention which formed the National Pharmacopœia, by the Rhode Island Medical Society, of which he was Vice President. He took an active part in the organization and proceedings of the Rhode Island Society for the Encouragement of Domestic Industry, before which he delivered addresses on several occasions. In 1824, in connection with his son, William Drowne, he published the Farmer's Guide, a comprehensive work on husbandry and gardening. He contributed various scientific and literary articles to the journals of the day, and participated in the proceedings of the American Academy of Arts and Sciences, and other learned bodies, of which he was a member. His *Lines to the Memory of Dr. Joseph Warren*, written shortly after the battle of Bunker Hill, are truly patriotic and evince the brotherly regard that existed between them professionally and as " Sons of Liberty."* During his life he delivered many botanical lectures, public orations and addresses, highly creditable to him as a man of refined taste and varied acquisitions, among which may be mentioned several commemorative of American

---

*Dr. Drowne's brother, Captain William Drowne, born April 17, 1755, (also one of that fraternity,) was with the shelled troops at Roxbury, on the day of the battle of Bunker Hill. In 1776 he was adjutant of Col. Bowen's regiment, of the Rhode Island Brigade, and in 1777 adjutant of Gen. Spencer's Brigade. The following year he embarked at Boston in a private sloop of war;—was an officer in various ships during several years and captured many vessels of the enemy. In 1781, his ship, the Belisarius, was taken by a British cruizer, carried to New York, when with other officers, he was transferred to the old Jersey prison ship. On being released, in 1783, he returned to his native place (Providence) with greatly impaired health. He died August 9, 1780.

Independence,—his *Eulogy on Washington, February 22,* 1800, and his *Oration in Aid of the Cause of the Greeks, Feb. 23, 1824.* The latter was delivered by the venerable orator at the First Baptist Meeting House, in Providence, when he was upwards of seventy years of age, with such remarkable fervor and pathos " that it was pronounced the most brilliant performance of his life."

ELIZABETH (RUSSELL) DROWNE lived in Boston until the breaking out of the Revolutionary war, when, with her brother Thomas, she came to Providence, and formed part of the family of her brother Jonathan Russell.[5] It was here that Dr. Drowne first saw her. There is much to show that Miss Russell appreciated the tastes of the Doctor and was worthy of his love. They were married at the residence of Jonathan Russell, who had removed to Holliston, Massachusetts, on Thanksgiving evening, 1777. Mrs. Drowne remained in Providence with her children while her husband was in Europe, in 1784-5, but accompanied him in 1792, in his journey through Virginia and Pennsylvania, which was then a comparative wilderness. She was fond of flowers and cultivated the choicest kinds, both in her house and garden.

ELIZA RUSSELL · DROWNE, daughter of Solomon Drowne, was born December 31, 1781, and died in Foster, April 30, 1865.

For upwards of half a century this lady manifested great interest in the botanical garden of her father at Mt. Hygeia. It contained at one time many rare flowers gathered from all parts of the world, and these were the objects of her constant care. It was at that period the most celebrated garden in the state, and people came long distances to see it.

She had also a talent for painting in water colors, and the evidences of her skill are carefully preserved in the family. Her flower pictures were used from time to time by Dr. Drowne to illustrate his lectures on Botany, when flowers were inaccessible or out of season. Miss Drowne cut numerous forms of paper pictures with scissors, as also curious watch papers with multitudes of birds, squirrels, flowers, trees, etc. Her artistic ability enabled her to represent almost any given subject with either pen or pencil, and she inherited to a remarkable degree a fondness for flowers.

Miss SARAH DROWNE, daughter of Dr. Drowne, was born September 10, 1790. She is the poetess of her father's family. In her early years she constructed verses with great versatility, and formerly recited (unwritten) poems of her composition which possessed much merit. This was her *forte* in the way of illustrating a particular subject, for she could readily improvise her thoughts and entertain for hours a select circle of friends. She had also great fondness for classic literature. An article in the Providence Journal of October 18, 1878, headed "FOSTER — MT. HYGEIA," however, takes off a little of the romantic spirit of the poetical, but adds to the practical realities of life, by stating that " Miss Drowne, who is the last surviving daughter of the late Dr. Drowne, and is now in her eighty-ninth year, has made this season (1878) with her own hands, at the old Drowne homestead, thirty cheeses. Beat this, who can ?" Bent with age and household cares, she still clings with tenacity to the old home and its long-time cherished associations from whence so many have passed away.

WILLIAM DROWNE, (son of *Dr. Drowne.*) clergyman and philanthropist, born in Morgantown, Monongalia county, West Virginia, October 26, 1793 ; died June 15, 1874; married, first, October 10, 1832, Mary Sprague, (daughter of Samuel Sprague and Ruhamah Borden, of Killingly, Connecticut,) born January 4, 1807; and died January 2, 1834.

Her child was:

    i. WILLIAM SPRAGUE DROWNE, born in Foster, November 14, 1833 ; died at sea, January 5, 1855.

He married, second, May 10, 1836, Emily Day, (daughter of Harvey Day and Olive Dorrance, of Killingly, Connecticut,) born April 28, 1810. Her four children were :

    ii. FRANCIS HERVEY DROWNE, born at Fruit Hill, North Providence, Rhode Island, October 16, 1837.

    iii. ELIZABETH RUSSELL DROWNE, born in Foster, Rhode Island, September 25, 1841.

    iv. EDGAR MERTON DROWNE, born in West Killingly, Connecticut, September 25, 1845 ; drowned at Cairo, Illinois, November 18, 1862. He died in the service of his country during the war of the Rebellion, and his name is enrolled on one of the bronze tablets of the Soldiers' and Sailors' Monument, in Exchange Place, Providence, Rhode Island.

    v. LUTHER WASHBURN DROWNE, clerk, etc., East Boston, Massachusetts, born at Danielsonville, Connecticut, July 14, 1850 ; married, November 5, 1874, Abbie Frances Rollins, (daughter of Samuel George Rollins and Lydia Maria Noble, of Biddeford, Maine) ; born May 7, 1852. Children : 1. *Emily Catharine*, born in East Boston, September 28, 1875. 2. *Elizabeth Russell*, born January 13, 1877. 3. *Edwin Lewis*, born May 18, 1878.

SOLOMON HORACE DROWNE, (son of Dr. Drowne,) agriculturist, of Woodstock, Connecticut, born in Union, Fayette county, Pennsylvania, August 26, 1796; died July 14, 1848; married, September 3, 1832, Susan Leonard, (daughter of Solomon Leonard and Sally Tucker,) of Taunton, Massachusetts.

Their children were :

1. SOPHIA ELIZABETH DROWNE, born in Foster, Rhode Island, March 27, 1833; died August 1, 1854; married, November 24, 1850, Henry Martin Rawson, born March 21, 1830. Children :

    i. CORNELIA LOUISA RAWSON, born September 30, 1851 : married August 10, 1869, Newton Chase Dana, Cashier of the Butchers and Drovers Bank, of Providence, Rhode Island; born September 11, 1848. Children : 1. *Mabel Louise Dana*, born March 22, 1870. 2. *Russell Newton Dana*, born October 21, 1873.

    ii. SOPHIA ELLEN RAWSON, born January 22, 1854.

2. ELLEN DOUGLASS DROWNE, born in Foster, March 13, 1835; married, March 16, 1865, Josiah Allen Blake, born January 9, 1811. Child :

    SARAH ELLEN BLAKE, born November 7, 1867.

3. SOLOMON DROWNE, clerk in National Bank of Commerce, in Providence, Rhode Island; born October 27, 1836; married, first, October 27, 1856, Maria Campbell, (daughter of Dr. William Henry Campbell and Esther Gallup,) born July 20, 1836; died September 23, 1868. Child :

    i. STELLA LOUISE DROWNE, born July 13, 1861.

He married, second, December 19, 1872, Amanda Malvina Cahoone, (daughter of Hoziel Cahoone and Prudence Andrews Weaver). Their child is :

    ii. MAUD CAHOONE DROWNE, born August 18, 1874.

4. THOMAS RUSSELL DROWNE, hardware merchant, Providence, Rhode Island. born August 13, 1838; married, March 23, 1863, Adelaide Aldrich Harrington, (daughter of Josiah Bennett Harrington and Huldah Maria Aldrich.) born May 18, 1845. Children :

    i. ADELAIDE VIRGINIA DROWNE, born January 11, 1864.

    ii. NELLIE DROWNE, born January 27, 1866 ; died October 9, 1867.

    iii. WALTER RUSSELL DROWNE, born December 31, 1869.

5. MARY LEONARD DROWNE, born July 13, 1840 ; married, December 11, 1862, Henry Augustus Harrington, born August 23, 1839. Children :

    i. ALICE ELIZA HARRINGTON, born October 14, 1863.

    ii. HARRY CLARK HARRINGTON, born November 3, 1866 ; died September 24, 1867.

    iii. CORNELIA DROWNE HARRINGTON, born December 25, 1876.

6. ADELAIDE VIRGINIA DROWNE, born March 15, 1842 ; died November 17, 1842.

7. EDWARD IRVING DROWNE, salesman, etc., Providence, Rhode Island, born October 25, 1843 ; married, June 11, 1873, Annie Louisa Brown, (daughter of John Esek Brown and Eliza Rhodes Arnold,) born January 28, 1847. Children :

    i. GEORGE LEONARD DROWNE, born April 26, 1874.

    ii. CLARA LOUISE DROWNE, born February 5, 1876 ; died January 28, 1878.

    iii. RUSSELL SEARS DROWNE, born May 11, 1877.

8. CHARLES HALL DROWNE, clerk in Providence, Rhode Island, born March 3, 1845 ; married, December 28, 1868, Hattie Adelaide Mansir, (daughter of William Mansir and Harriet Hallet). Children :

    i. HATTIE ISABEL DROWNE, born September 30, 1871 ; died May 7, 1872.

    ii. DAISY ISABEL DROWNE, born October 9, 1874.

9. SARAH CORNELIA DROWNE, born June 10, 1847; married, December 2, 1875, Frederick Goodwin Hagan, born September 6, 1849. Child:

SUSAN DROWNE HAGAN, born June 1, 1877.

HENRY BERNARDIN DROWNE, (son of Dr. *Solomon* and *Elizabeth [Russell] Drowne*⁵; of *Thomas Russell,*⁴) born at Union, Fayette county, Pennsylvania, April 6, 1799; died February 7, 1873; married Julia Ann, daughter of Thomas and Polly (Rhodes) Stafford, of Warwick, Rhode Island, April 24, 1821. She was born June 5, 1802.

Early in life, while residing with his father, in Foster, he devoted himself to agriculture. In 1823 he purchased land and built a house at Fruit Hill, North Providence, where he lived for the next twenty-five years. In 1835, conjointly with his sisters, he founded the Fruit Hill Classical Institute, which was attended with success. His interests in Providence being large, he erected the house at 127 Benefit street, to which he removed in 1850. His time was chiefly occupied in the management of several estates and other financial trusts, in which he was noted for his probity and sagacious conclusions. At an early date he became connected with the Rhode Island Society for the Encouragement of Domestic Industry, and ever took a prominent part in its management. His kindly spirit was obvious in many unostentatious acts of benevolence.

They had seven children, as follows:

1. HENRY THAYER DROWNE, (of New York,) born at Woodstock, Connecticut, March 25, 1822, married, December 24, 1851, Sarah Rhodes Arnold, (daughter of

Henry T. Drowne

George Carpenter Arnold and Phebe Rhodes, of Providence, Rhode Island,) born March 2, 1832.   Only son:

HENRY RUSSELL DROWNE, born in New York City, August 31, 1860.

HENRY THAYER DROWNE took up his residence in New York in 1841; was clerk for several years, latterly in the commission house of C. Fiske Harris.   In 1861 was one of the originators, with the Rev. Dr. Francis Vinton, Benjamin G. Arnold, Charles H. Russell, George William Curtis, and others, of the "*Sons of Rhode Island, in New York,*" and its latest Secretary.

For twenty-four years Mr. Drowne has been an officer of the "Old" National Fire Insurance Company in the city of New York; first as Secretary and latterly as President. He is First Vice President of the New York Genealogical and Biographical Society, and Librarian of the American Ethnological Society; Life-member of the New York Historical Society, and of the New England Society of New York; Fellow of the American Geographical Society, and Corresponding Member of the New England Historic-Genealogical Society, and the Historical Societies of Rhode Island, Pennsylvania, Wisconsin, Vermont, and Chicago. He is also member of the Society of Cincinnati, in Rhode Island, being the oldest grandson of Dr. Solomon Drowne, of the Revolutionary Army, (of which society Major-General Nathanael Greene was first President).

2.   THOMAS STAFFORD DROWNE, D. D., born at Fruit Hill, North Providence, Rhode Island, July 9, 1823; married, first, April 13, 1852, Anne Catherine Beatty,

(daughter of Robert Beatty and Cathrine Louisa Armstrong, of Brooklyn, New York,) who was born September 12, 1833, and died April 19, 1860.

Their only child is :

   i. THOMAS STAFFORD DROWNE, JR., Columbia College, New York, class 1877, A. B., and Columbia Law School, class 1879, LL. B., born July 12, 1857.

He married, second, July 15, 1869, Georgiana Morgan, (daughter of Nathan Denison Morgan and Mary Brown Churchill, of Brooklyn, Long Island,) born September 10, 1848.   Children :

   ii. HELEN LOUISA DROWNE, born May 18, 1871.

   iii. LEONARD BERNARDIN DROWNE, born Sept. 29, 1875.

DR. DROWNE graduated at Brown University in 1845; and at the General Theological Seminary, New York, in 1848; was admitted to priest's orders July 1, 1849, in the Church of the Holy Trinity, Brooklyn Heights, by Bishop Whittingham, of Maryland.   On the first of November, 1848, he became Assistant Minister of the same church, in which position he continued nearly ten years.   In 1848 he was elected to the rectorship of St. Paul's parish, Brooklyn, where he remained seventeen years, during which time a new church was erected.   On the first of August, 1878, he removed to Garden City, L. I., having been appointed Dean of the Divinity School on the Cathedral Foundation, and Minister in charge of the services at that place.

Since the erection of Long Island into a Diocese, Dr. Drowne has filled the office of its Secretary, and, in 1870, he was appointed the Registrar and Historiog-

rapher of the Diocese. His interest in historical and antiquarian researches has led to his election to membership in several State historical societies, the American Ethnological Society, etc.

Dr. Drowne has made architecture a study, and was associated with the late Minard Lafever, in the preparation of "The Architectural Instructor," containing a history of architecture, of which he wrote the letter-press. He also published "A Commemorative Discourse on the Completion of the Church of the Holy Trinity, December 19, 1867"; and an "Address at a Memorial Service, November 26, 1871," on the occasion of uncovering the mural tablet erected in memory of its founders. From time to time he has contributed articles, theological, critical, and historical, to various reviews.

3. SOLOMON DROWNE, born May 1; died May 4, 1825.

4. LOUISA DROWNE, born August 3, 1827; died December 26, 1846.

5. CHRISTOPHER RHODES DROWNE, Cashier of the Liberty Bank, Treasurer of the Merchants Savings Bank, also of the Swan Point Cemetery, Providence; born June 7, 1830; married, December 4, 1861, Alice Wheeler Peabody, (daughter of William Bailey Peabody and Lydia Braman, of Newport, Rhode Island,) born July 25, 1842. Children:

   i. PASCHAL BRAMAN DROWNE, born October 20, 1862.
   ii. LOUISA RHODES DROWNE, born December 12, 1864.
   iii. ROBERT SEAMAN DROWNE, born July 26, 1866; died August 24, 1868.

iv. CHRISTOPHER LEONARD DROWNE, born March 20, 1869; died July 11, 1871.

v. ALICE ELIZABETH DROWNE, born July 19, 1871.

vi. CHRISTOPHER STAFFORD DROWNE, born July 5. 1874.

vii. ROBERT HOLDEN DROWNE, born December 14, 1877.

6. GEORGE RUSSELL DROWNE, merchant of Providence, Rhode Island, born May 14, 1835; married, first, November 5, 1855, Mary Ann Simmons, (daughter of Valentine Simmons and Mary Ann Lombard, of Little Compton, Rhode Island,) born August 7, 1835; died February 21, 1863. Children:

i. GEORGE RUSSELL DROWNE, JR., born January 24, 1857.

ii. JULIA STAFFORD DROWNE, born April 8, 1861.

He married, second, November 25, 1868, Josephine Alvina Simmons. (sister of the first wife,) born August 1, 1841. Children:

iii. MARIE ANTOINETTE DROWNE, born in Boston, November 26. 1869; died in Providence, June 12, 1877.

iv. WILFRED SIMMONS DROWNE, born in Providence, March 30, 1875.

v. ETHEL LINCOLN DROWNE, born in Little Compton, September 25, 1876.

7. JULIA ANNE DROWNE, born March 23, 1837; died March 26, 1837.

The children of Henry B. Drowne, with the exception of the oldest son, were born at Fruit Hill, North Providence, Rhode Island.

www.ingramcontent.com/pod-product-compliance
Lightning Source LLC
Chambersburg PA
CBHW021454090426
42739CB00009B/1746